FLIGHTS
of
FANCY

FLIGHTS
of
FANCY

Maxine Lantz

WESTBOW
PRESS
A DIVISION OF THOMAS NELSON

WestBow Press books may be ordered through booksellers or by contacting:

WestBow Press
A Division of Thomas Nelson
1663 Liberty Drive
Bloomington, IN 47403
www.westbowpress.com
1-(866) 928-1240

Because of the dynamic nature of the Internet, any web addresses or links contained in this book may have changed since publication and may no longer be valid. The views expressed in this work are solely those of the author and do not necessarily reflect the views of the publisher, and the publisher hereby disclaims any responsibility for them.

Certain stock imagery © Thinkstock.
Any people depicted in stock imagery provided by Thinkstock are models, and such images are being used for illustrative purposes only.

ISBN: 978-1-4497-5594-2 (e)
ISBN: 978-1-4497-5593-5 (sc)

Library of Congress Control Number: 2012910285

Printed in the United States of America

WestBow Press rev. date: 9/21/2012

AUTHOR'S FOREWORD

I have called this booklet of poetry "Flights of Fancy" because I think that the change Christ made in my life is symbolized by the butterfly that changes from a chrysalis to a thing of great beauty.

I hope that these poems will give you some insight into what I believe is the true character of God and his son, Jesus Christ. I thank God for saving me, and I look forward to spending eternity with God and Jesus Christ.

I pray that these poems will edify the reader, and that those who know Christ as Saviour will be encouraged to continue their walk with him. For the reader that does not yet know Christ in this personal way, I pray that these words will lead you to the point in your life where you will accept Christ as your personal Saviour.

I would also like to take this opportunity to thank the keepers of my words. Each poem I write gets sent to my sister (Lynda Taylor), my husband Jim, my pastor and his wife (John & Cheryl Scorgie, who are also dear friends), and to another two friends (Carrol Ross and Joyce Lindsay). They are my biggest supporters, and I thank them for their love, loyalty and faithfulness.

Thank-you,
Maxine Lantz

Other Books By This Author:

Rhyming Revelation
Love On The Wing
Covenant Of Care
Basking In The Son-Shine
Abundant Life

CONTENTS

A NEW ROAD

A new road lies before me;
Its end I cannot view.
Will it be full of twists and turns?
I do not have a clue.
No footprints mar its surface;
The top is smooth as glass.
How will it change when I move on
And time has flown and passed?
How many people will I meet
Along this new road's way?
Will they walk on renewed in heart
For words I had to say?
Will they know that I love the Lord?
Will they wonder at it all?
Will they too yield up their own life
And on My Savior call?
Will there be hidden dangers there
And snares to grab my feet?
Will I only travel half the length
Before my trip's complete?
Oh, Lord, each day I walk this path
I ask you linger near,
For I know when you walk nearby,
I won't doubt and I won't fear.
And when my journey's over,
And I look back at the road,
Will I have walked God's narrow way
Or on the world's path strode?
Oh, Lord, I ask you. Help me, please,
To not turn left or right,
To stay upon your narrow way
As I stay within your sight.
And when the road comes to an end,
And I walk life's path no more,
Then may I see your precious face
As I enter heaven's door.

A SERVANT IN CHRIST

She opened the door and met me
With her arms both open wide
And welcomed me with a big, big hug
That made me feel warm inside.
Then I felt the soft arms of the woman
Turn to arms of power and might.
'Twas the arms of Jesus Christ, my Lord.
I'll not soon forget that night.
I watched as she made biscuits
That just melted in your mouth.
She added jam and poured the tea.
A real king's feast, no doubt.
Then I saw the soft hands of the woman
Turn to calloused nail-scarred hands –
The hands of Christ, my Saviour –
Son of God and Son of Man.
I watched as she reached over
And gave a treat to the little boy.
The mother's heartfelt "thank-you"
Echoed the little boy's joy.
Then I saw the eyes of the woman
Turn to the eyes of Jesus Christ
That had seen that mother's frustration
As the young boy her patience tried.
I watched as she held the shoulders
While the woman cried her tears.
She had known the woman's happy words
Hid all her misery and fears.
Then I saw the ears of the woman
Take the form of those of the Lord,
And I knew that the whole experience
Had really changed my world.
For I knew then that hospitality
In all of its shapes and forms
Meant nothing at all unless it is based
On the love of Christ, the Lord.

ANGEL UNAWARE

Only a few last-minute shoppers rushed past me on the nearly-deserted street, and I thought of my family waiting for me at home. I had told my wife that I would be a "little" late, but that "little" had turned into over four hours.

The wind was bitingly cold, and I was pleased that I had a thick sweater on under my wool coat. Even so, I turned my collar up to retain some extra heat against the cold.

I almost never noticed him. Sitting on a pile of cardboard, with his back pressed up against the wall in the alley, he too sought relief from the bitterly cold wind. I had glanced down the alley as I passed it, and normally I would have hurried past without even considering him. But something in his eyes caught my attention.

He nodded to me as I passed, and I felt compelled to go up to him. He asked, "Hey, Mister, could you spare a few dollars so that I could get something to eat?" Looking closer at him, I noticed that his jacket was threadbare, torn and very dirty. It was definitely not suitable to keep anyone warm, especially with the extremely cold wind.

Then, I did something totally out of character. I took off my jacket and offered it to him. At first, he told me that he didn't need it. When I insisted, he finally took it and put it on over his own jacket. He sighed as the warmth returned to his body, and I asked him if he wanted to walk to the diner to get a meal – my treat, of course. He reluctantly agreed, and we walked the block to the diner together.

As we shared a meal of meat loaf and potatoes, he told me that his name was Mike, and that he had fallen on hard times. And then, he asked me if I knew the Lord. I told him that I had known the Lord for about five years. Then he asked "Do you love the Lord above all else? Is your love for him real in your life?" I pondered those questions, and had to admit to myself, and to Mike, that in the last year of so, I had not put God first in my life as I pursued business success. I also admitted that I had not put my family second in my life in the pursuit of that same financial goal.

Mike shed a tear as I told him those facts, and said that he would pray for me. He would be praying that I would be able to set the right priorities in my life. I awkwardly thanked him for that, and we prepared to leave.

Dusk was falling as we retraced our steps to the alley where we had first met. Mike handed my coat back. He said that he would be fine now, and wouldn't be needing it. I tried to tell him that he could keep it, but he declined my offer.

I watched as he walked down the street away from me. Then I noticed a small bit of white hanging from the bottom of his torn, threadbare jacket. Why it looked like . . . . . feathered wings! Could this be a trick of the light, or something else? I called to him and ran to where I had seen him disappear into the ever-deepening dusk. He was nowhere to be seen!

Immediately, I remembered the verse in the Bible about entertaining angels unaware. Could it be? Could Mike be an angel? I guess that I will never know or understand – was I an angel sent for Mike or was he an angel sent for me?

Those questions haunted me all the way home. When I reached home, I thanked God for the family he had given me, and asked him to help me be a better husband and father. I also asked him to help me draw closer to him and his son, Jesus Christ. And I asked his blessings on Mike, unconcerned whether he was an angel or not, knowing that it did not matter anymore.

BE KIND AND FORGIVE

*"Be kind and compassionate to one another, forgiving
each other, just as in Christ God forgave you."*

Ephesians 4:32 NIV

Be kind and compassionate to all that you meet.
Forgive all the hurts that occur.
Forgive as the Father forgave you in Christ,
Who died so salvation's ensured.
There is no limit on the number of times
That we must decide to forgive.
Just do what the Bible tells us we must do
And in Jesus continue to live.
For Christ, on the cross, forgave all the ones
Who, with derision, His holy name scorned.
He forgave his tormentors who struck with the scourge
And crowned Him with those cruel thorns.
We cannot do less than to model our lives
On the one without sin who hung there.
For each drop of His blood as it fell on the ground
Was the witness to how much He cared.
So, when life brings a sense of betrayal or hurt
You can't let revenge win the day.
For Christ, who had suffered his death on the cross
Said forgiveness is the only way.
So, be kind and compassionate to all that you meet.
Forgive all the hurts that occur.
Forgive as the Father forgave you in Christ,
And eternity will be yours, for sure.

BECAUSE I LOVE GOD'S LAW

"Great peace have they who love your law,
and nothing can make them stumble."

Psalm 119:165 NIV

Great peace have we who love God's law
For naught can make us fall.
In times of great distress, I know
That God's my all in all.
There is no principality,
No man, no king, no throne
Can cause my feet to stumble
For I never stand alone.
My mighty God is always near
To comfort and to guide,
And Satan's demons have no power
When God is by my side.
When Satan tries to tangle me
And tries to make me fall,
I need to call on God alone;
He'll always hear my call.
He'll vanquish all my enemies,
Each day and any hour.
I know that He will be right there
In majesty and power.
He'll comfort me forever
With a love that will not cease,
And because I love His holy law,
My God will grant me peace.

BLESSINGS FOR OBEDIENCE

"The LORD will establish you as his holy people, as he promised you on oath, if you keep the commands of the LORD your God and walk in his ways. Then all the peoples on earth will see that you are called by the name of the LORD, and they will fear you. The LORD will grant you abundant prosperity—in the fruit of your womb, the young of your livestock and the crops of your ground—in the land he swore to your forefathers to give you. The LORD will open the heavens, the storehouse of his bounty, to send rain on your land in season and to bless all the work of your hands. You will lend to many nations but will borrow from none. ¹³ The LORD will make you the head, not the tail. If you pay attention to the commands of the LORD your God that I give you this day and carefully follow them, you will always be at the top, never at the bottom. ¹⁴ Do not turn aside from any of the commands I give you today, to the right or to the left, following other gods and serving them.

Deuteronomy 28:9-14 NIV

If you fully obey the Lord and His ways,
All the commands that He has set forth,
Then the Lord, your God, will set you up high
Above all the nations of earth.

All the blessings of God will come upon you
And will shower you throughout your days.
If you only obey all the precepts He taught
And you daily walk in His ways.

You'll be blessed in the city and country too
And your foes who rise up will not win.
The Lord will bestow His great blessings on you
As you go out and you go in.

Whatever you put your hand to in life
Will be blessed by the Father above,
As you follow His ways in your daily walk
And to others display God's great love.

7

And the Father will pour out his great bounty;
There's no end to heaven's great store.
If you will only put your trust in Christ,
His blessings will outpour.

And God in His great love for His children
Will send the rain to water your land,
And His blessings continue throughout your life
As you rest in His mighty hand.

Do not serve any god that has no power to save.
From God's commands do not turn aside.
And the blessings you'll see will astound and amaze
As in God's gracious love you abide.

CHOOSE THIS DAY

*But if serving the LORD seems undesirable to
you, then choose for yourselves this day whom you
will serve, whether the gods your ancestors served
beyond the Euphrates, or the gods of the Amorites,
in whose land you are living. But as for me and
my household, we will serve the LORD.""*

Joshua 24:15 NIV

Each man must choose his master,
The one on whom he'll serve-
A god of wood or metal
That can't see or utter words
Or the God of might and glory
Whose creation's all around.
The God in whom all goodness
And righteousness is found.

The choice is somewhat daunting
For eternity's at stake.
The place our spirits spend all time
Depends on choices made.
So each must think and ponder
And weigh the bad and good –
A God of love and mercy
Or an idol made of wood?

The answer's easy as I see,
No other one is true –
I'll choose the God of glory
No matter what men do.
I'll stand firm just like Joshua
And all will hear these words,
"But as for me and my house,
We will choose to serve the Lord".

CHRIST IN ME

"I have been crucified with Christ and I no longer live, but Christ lives in me. The life I live in the body, I live by faith in the Son of God, who loved me and gave himself for me."

Galatians 2:20 NIV

With Christ, I've been crucified
On the cross with my King.
It's not I that lives each day;
For I now live in Him.
I dwell in mortal body
But my source is faith in God
And in His son, Lord Jesus,
I can only give them laud.
For all that they've done for me,
I humbly give them praise.
Christ loves me and He daily gives
His mercy and His grace.
His love extended to the cross,
That cruel Golgotha tree,
When, to fulfill His father's plan
He hung and died for me.
My sin was all atoned for,
My life was made brand new
In love, He took my offered heart
And He can do the same for you.
Just ask believing what He'll do
And confess your sinful heart,
His peace, and joy and love are yours
And from you will not depart.

COME, LET US BOW DOWN IN WORSHIP

*Come, let us bow down in worship, let us kneel before
the LORD our Maker; for he is our God and we are
the people of his pasture, the flock under his care.*

Come, and let us bow down in praise;
Let us kneel before our great Lord.
He's our Creator and our King
As it says throughout God's own word.
He is our God for time to come.
He was here before time began.
He ordained ere the earth had form
His redeeming salvation plan.
We are the sheep of his pasture,
The flock that is under His care.
Our lives have import to our God
And, for us, He is always there.
So, come, let us worship Him daily.
Let us send up a chorus of praise.
He is our Maker; He is our God.
Let us praise him for all our days.

DEAR JESUS

Just thought that I would write and thank you for your wonderful gift. I never expected to have such a wonderful gift given to me because I wasn't really worthy of such a gift. However, because you gave me this great gift, I now feel worthy of receiving it. Kinda funny how that worked out, isn't it?

I've read how you were accused by the religious leaders of your time for claiming to be a king and for not paying taxes to Caesar. If those rulers had only heard you say "Render unto Caesar what is Caesar's and unto God what is God's", they would have known that tax charge was false. As for the other charge, you were only stating the truth when you said that you were a king. Why couldn't they see that?

I know that this gift involved great sacrifice and pain. I heard how they beat you and made you carry that heavy cross all the way to Calvary. And how you fell under the load. Then they nailed your hands and feet to that wooden cross. I am so sorry that you suffered such pain for my sins.

The story about the two thieves that were on either side of you as you hung on that cross has been circulating these many years. How the one thief sneeringly ordered you to save yourself as well as him and the other thief. Imagine talking like that to the King of kings! Then, I heard that the second thief clarified the facts for the first one. He told him that both of them were being punished justly for their deeds, but that you were innocent. Then he asked you to remember him when you come into your kingdom, and you promised him that he would be in paradise with you that very day. What great joy that must have given him! I know how I felt when you promised me that same promise of eternity spent with you.

Joseph of Arimathea was a good friend to you. After you had died, he asked Pilate if he could have your body for burial. He even used his new unused tomb for your burial. What a good friend! I hope that I can be as good a friend to those people that you put in my life.

I can't imagine how sad all of your friends must have been when you were crucified. After all, they had spent most of the years of your ministry here on earth with you. I know how sad I would be without you in my life!

Now here's the best part of the gift you gave me- the tomb is empty! You didn't stay dead! You arose on the third day in power and might. You beat the grave and death no longer has victory. Because of your Death and Resurrection, I have the quiet assurance that I will share eternity with you and your Father.

With this wonderful gift in my possession, I will share it with as many people as I can before you call me home.

In gratitude,
A Redeemed Sinner

DENY, PICK UP AND FOLLOW

Deny thyself, and pick up my cross
And daily follow me.
I'll grant you all your heart's desires
And your soul's liberty.

My way is narrow and the gate
Is small if you compare
The path the world wanders on;
They have a broad path there.

The gate for them is very large
And many may go in,
But on the foretold judgment day
They'll know judgment for their sin.

So, daily my disciple be
And to the world show
How great my love is for them all
So other folks will know

The mercy, joy and peace and love
And my all-providing care
Bestowed on those repentant hearts
Who speak the sinner's prayer.

My way is not an easy one
For when you will be seen
As one of my disciples,
Your troubles will be keen.

But I will walk right by your side;
You'll never be alone.
I'll guide you in each step you take
For I love you. You're my own.

And when your soul slips from this earth
And soars to heights above,
We'll share that quiet communion
And you'll rest within my love.

But while on earth you must deny
In each moment of each day,
The self that rises up within
And, if you will obey,

Then great will be your just reward
When your time on earth is gone,
For you will hear me say in love,
"Well done, my Child, well done."

DID ADAM KNOW?

Did Adam know with that first bite
That he had doomed mankind
To die without the Savior's grace?
Just what was on his mind?
The fruit looked good and tasty, too,
And Adam took a bite.
This act of disobedience
Would cause mankind to die.
And when the fruit had passed his lips,
He noticed they were bare.
They hid from Christ in Eden
As they heard Him walking there.
Did Adam know that that first sin
Would doom mankind to be
Ensured of lasting life in hell?
That was the penalty!
The only thing that gave a hope
Would be a sacrifice
Just like the lamb Christ slayed for them,
Christ would yield up His life.
And that first bloodshed would foretell
Christ's time upon the cross.
For Christ would shed His blood for us
To save our souls from loss.
Did Adam know the joy that rises
In a soul that has been saved?
Could he give thanks to Christ, his Lord,
For rescue from the grave?
Did he, with truly contrite heart,
Ask Jesus to forgive
And know the peace and joy Christ brings,
Throughout the days he lived?
And when his time on earth was done,
Did his soul know heaven's place?
And did He bow at Jesus' feet
When he met Him face-to-face?

GIVE THANKS

*"Be joyful always; pray continually; give
thanks in all circumstances, for this is
God's will for you in Christ Jesus."*

1 Thessalonians 5:16-18 NIV

Be joyful in all things for this is God's way
In all times and places, continue to pray.
Give thanks for the roses and for the thorns too.
Give thanks for the trials that may worry you.
Give thanks for the sunshine and thanks for the rain.
Give thanks for the pleasure and also the pain.
Give thanks for the darks times and times in full sun,
Give thanks for the work in your life that God's done.
Give thanks for salvation and dark sins atoned.
Give thanks for the fact that you won't walk alone.
Give thanks for God's mercy, His love and His grace.
Give thanks that you rest in God's tender embrace.
Give thanks for His word that shows us how to live.
Give thanks for the hope that salvation does give.
Give thanks and look forward to heav'n in God's time.
Give thanks for eternal communion divine.
Be joyful in all things for this is God's way
In all times and places, continue to pray.

GOD HAS GIVEN A GREAT GIFT

For the Spirit God gave us does not make us timid,
but gives us power, love and self-discipline

2 Timothy 1:7 NIV

God has given us a great gift-
On us He has bestowed
The Holy Spirit's presence.
Our body's His abode.

Our body is the temple
Where the Holy Spirit resides.
He'll daily live within us;
He'll instruct us and He'll guide.

With the Spirit's holy presence,
We have no need to fear
And cower when the Enemy
Threatens and draws near.

We'll stand in Christ's own power
Availed to us each day
If we will simply trust Him
And walk His narrow way.

And the Spirit will be with us
To teach us and to show
If there is something that is wrong
Or if we lack in self-control.

The gift that we've been given –
The Holy Spirit within –
Is beyond man's comprehension
Unless he's been cleansed from sin.

GOD-GIVEN GRACE

*"...who has saved us and called us to a holy life—not
because of anything we have done but because of
his own purpose and grace. This grace was given
us in Christ Jesus before the beginning of time,"*

2 Timothy 1:9 NIV

Jesus called us to a holy life
As a result of being saved.
Not because of what we've done
But because of his purpose and grace.

Long before the earth had its form
And before we ever drew breath,
Christ Jesus bestowed his grace on us.
Our salvation destroyed our death.

Grace was given in measure full
Unbounded by human design,
Given freely when a repentant heart
On Jesus' great name cries.

Nothing man can do on earth
Will ever diminish the power
Of Christ's great grace to change a life
In that real salvation hour.

So, live a life of righteousness
As Christ has said to do,
And God will be pleased and pour out
His many blessings on you.

GOD'S PLAN FOR CHRISTMAS

In a far-off place, before time began
God, the Father, told his Son the plan
To save mankind from certain death.
He asked of Christ this grave request.

"Oh, most beloved son of mine,
I ask you leave this place divine.
On earth, you'll take the form of man.
That's just the start of redemption's plan.
In a lowly stable, you'll be born
As a helpless babe, on a Christmas morn.
And when you make your way to earth
Heavenly choirs will proclaim your birth.
Shepherds abiding in the night
Will go to Bethlehem to catch a sight
Of the earth's Redeemer, King and Lord.
All things foretold in my Holy Word.
You'll grow in knowledge and do my task.
For me, my Son, this is so hard to ask!

You'll heal the sick, and cure the lame –
All things performed in my holy name.
The dead will rise, the blind will see.
You'll lead the people's praise to me."
And then God said, with a tear in his eye,
"It pains me, Son, for you'll have to die.
You'll be bruised and beaten, and then you'll be
Nailed to the cross on dark Calvary.
Your blood will flow and atone for the sin
So that poor flawed man may enter in
To share in heaven eternal days.
I do not know of a better way.
You'll go to earth to save sinful man.
What do you think of redemption's plan?"

"O, Father, please know I'll pay the cost.
I know, without it, man is lost.
I'll go to earth and I'll be laid
In a stable low, on a bed of hay.
I'll hear the heavenly choirs sing
And the Magi too, when their presents they bring.
I'll preach your love and redemptive plan
To save each child, each woman, man.
And though I know I'll suffer the cross
I'll pay the price to save man from loss.
My blood, for all sin, will ever atone.
I'll die... I'll rise... and then come home
To sit forever at your right hand,
To intercede between you and man."

So, Friends, today as we remember Christ's birth,
Remember how he willingly came down to earth
To fulfill his father's redemptive plan
That is all we need to understand.

Thank you, Jesus, for bearing my shame.
I'm a child of the King, and I carry his name.
No power on earth can ever take me away.
And it all started back on that first Christmas day.

GOD'S PROMISES

Do not fear, for I am with you.
And from you I'll not depart.
I will be your God forever;
You're the apple of my heart.
I will strengthen and sustain you
And uphold you with my hand.
When the world makes you stumble,
I will always help you stand.
Know there is no king or kingdom
That can ever loose my grasp
For you're precious to me, my child,
And my love for you will last.
Child, there is no time or distance
That can separate us now.
And in times of trial and tempting
You'll have access to my power.
With a whisper or a loud shout,
When you call upon my name,
I will hear and I will answer
And my precious child sustain.
So, remember that I've told you
That I always will be near,
So please don't ever doubt me.
Don't dismay and do not fear.

HE IS LORD

The world says that there is no God,
That god resides within.
But that cannot help sin-stained man
To free him from his sin.

What power can man, with feeble strength,
Display and sin atone?
That power, in all its majesty,
Is held by God alone.

What man can breathe the world to life,
And set the stars in place?
God can; He did the world create
And set it out in space.

And who can shape a tiny babe
Beneath its mother's heart?
God can, and in His infinite love,
Has loved each from the start.

And man thinks that he knows it all;
He needs not God's control.
But, woe to him who curses God,
For he's sure to lose his soul.

There'll come a time when all on earth
Will bow and then proclaim
That Christ is Lord, and Lord alone,
And tremble at His name.

Believers know this as a fact
That Christ is lord of all,
And know His grace and mercy too
When on His name they call.

They bow today in gratitude
For His wisdom and His grace
And look ahead to glory time
When they'll see Him face-to-face.

They comprehend they're feeble
When on their own power they stand
But know the power availed to them
As they rest within Christ's hand.

No king or principality,
No throne or kingdom known
Will ever know omnipotent power
As is found before God's throne.

The power to transform sin-stained lives,
And redeem man from his sin
As a soul once chained to Satan's plan
Begins life free again.

And when Satan prowls around and tries
To make us doubt and fear,
Our power resides in knowing
That our Savior's always near.

We know that Satan has not won;
He doesn't have the power
Because of Calvary's sacrifice
And Christ's resurrection hour.

So, when men say there is no God,
I know that they are wrong
For to my mighty Savior,
My cleansed soul now belongs.

HEARTS SHARED

When my soul wings its way to heaven,
I will not be alone.
I'll carry with me bits and pieces
Of all the ones I've known.

For each time that I meet a soul
For a season or a time,
I give a piece of myself to them
And a piece of them is mine.

It may be just a smile or word
Encouraging to say,
But when two souls by God-chance meet
A piece of each heart stays.

The piece I give won't often match
The piece I get in kind.
Each piece I get is grafted to
My heart, and fits just fine.

And when I stand beside my Lord
I know I'll hear Him say,
"It's not how much you got from them,
But how much you gave away."

HEAVENLY WISDOM

*But the wisdom that comes from heaven is first of all
pure; then peace-loving, considerate, submissive, full of
mercy and good fruit, impartial and sincere. Peacemakers
who sow in peace reap a harvest of righteousness."*

James 3:17-18 NIV

Heaven's wisdom is not sullied
Or defiled; it is pure.
It shows to all the love of peace.
Of this, you can be sure.

Consideration is what's shown
When wisdom is applied.
It is submissive to God's laws
As we in Him abide.

It's full of mercy and good fruit,
Impartial and sincere.
We all should strive to gain this prize;
This, to us, should be clear.

And those who sow in peace will see
A righteous harvest given,
For they applied God's great decrees
And gained wisdom from heaven.

HOLY SPIRIT, GENTLE SPIRIT

A gentle spirit's what I pray.
Please help me, Lord, from day to day.
I know that only with your grace
With victory, each day's course I'll race.
And when sun sets, my voice I'll raise
To you my song of thankful praise.

Lord, let me share my earthly things
With those your Spirit to me brings
Let me ensure, and take great care,
To love your people, unaware
Of creed or colour, wealth or fame.
I'll do it all in your dear name.

Lord, as I walk my path in life,
I'll need your help as mother/wife.
So still the words sharp on my tongue
And help me not one soul to wrong.
So that the world will watch and see
I walk with you; you walk with me.

I know without you I am naught.
Help me to know my win you've bought
By hanging on Golgotha's tree -
Bleeding, dieing, saving me.
So, Jesus Lord, please help me say
"I walked with God" at end of day.

HOSANNA

Hosanna to the King of Kings,
The one who made all earthly things -
The things that fly, crawl, walk and swim.
Our praise should always rise to Him.

Hosanna to the Lord of Lords,
Who calmed the wind just by His words.
The demons trembled as He neared,
For His great power and might they feared.

Hosanna to the Three in One –
The Father, Holy Spirit, Son.
The mystery of one of three
May be explained when Christ we see.

HUMBLE YOURSELVES BEFORE THE LORD

"Humble yourselves before the Lord,
and he will lift you up."

James 4:10 NIV

Humble yourselves before the Lord.
Come to Him with hearts of praise.
Let your heart be full of your gratitude,
And humble hosannas raise.
Approach His holy throne of grace
And humbly prostrate fall.
Acknowledge Him as Lord and King
For He is your all in all.
Let not the world keep you away
For Jesus should come first.
He'll take away your hunger
And satisfy your thirst.
For when you humbly approach Him,
The Lord will lift you up,
And when you show it empty,
Living water will fill your cup.
So daily walk on the narrow way
And feed each day on God's Word
And blessings will flow from the throne of God
When you humbly approach the Lord.

I DO BELIEVE

I do believe that the triune God
Is Father, Spirit, Son -
The mystery of three distinct parts,
And yet the three are one.

Not one part is raised higher
Than the other parts you see.
Each part has a specific task
To save both you and me.

The Father made salvation's plan.
The Son fulfilled God's will.
The Holy Spirit is our guide;
He indwells and our soul fills.

I do believe that Jesus Christ,
The Son of God, most high,
Came down to earth as a helpless babe
And on Calvary's cross did die.

He lived, like us, upon this earth;
He was tempted and had trials.
His actions proved that He is God
For by sin, He was not defiled.

He left the glory of the heavens
And His father's own right hand.
He suffered death upon the cross
According to God's plan.

I do believe Christ rose again;
Death could not win that fight.
Christ rose in all His splendor,
His majesty and might.

The world thought they'd done him in;
No longer him they'd see.
But Jesus' resurrection day
Fulfilled all prophecy.

Death could not hold Him in the grave;
The grave gave up its power
When Christ's full deity was shown
In that resurrection hour.

I do believe my soul is saved
For I've called upon Christ's name.
And confessed to Him my sin-filled state
And his grace and mercy claimed.

I now enjoy His peace and joy
As each new day arrives.
Because He died on Calvary's cross
My soul is now alive.

IF MY PEOPLE

*"If my people, who are called by my name, will humble
themselves and pray and seek my face and turn from
their wicked ways, then will I hear from heaven and
will forgive their sin and will heal their land."*

2 Chronicles 7:14 NIV

If my people, who are called by my name,
Will humble themselves and show me no shame,
I will hear all their cries and their sins will forgive.
In the midst of my love they will forever live.

If my people, who are called by my name,
Will pray to my Father, and his promises claim,
I will give them abundance in their lives every day
If they will but repent and follow my way.

If my people, who are called by my name,
Will just seek my face and shun glory and fame,
I will show them my great love while they walk this earth,
And when up in heaven, how great is their worth.

If my people, who are called by my name,
Will remember my power in healing the lame,
I'll use that same power and by my outstretched hand,
I'll fulfill my promise and I'll heal their land.

I KNOW MY REDEEMER LIVES

*I know that my redeemer lives, and that in
the end he will stand on the earth.*

Job 19.25 NIV

I know that my Redeemer lives
And, on this earth, He'll stand.
The day that He comes back again
Will be glorious and grand.

He will not come in flesh and blood
As when He walked this earth;
He won't come helpless as a babe
As on the morning of His birth.

He'll come in power and majesty,
In control of all He sees.
Where'er He looks, the people there
Will be falling on their knees.

Their voices will proclaim Him Lord,
Against their will or not,
And all believers will rejoice
That their souls, with blood, He bought.

He'll be the King of majesty;
All prophecies fulfilled.
The world that He created
Will watch in wonder, quiet and still.

My soul awaits that wondrous time.
Though I can't truly comprehend,
I know that my Redeemer lives
And will rule on earth again.

I'LL NEVER KNOW

An unclean sinner, full of sin,
And yet You chose to take me in.

You lifted me from deep despair
And saved me with Your gracious care.

I'll never know what made you say
"You'll be a child of Mine today."

But evermore my song will be
Ten thousand praises, all for Thee.

So thank you, Lord, for ransomed soul
You cleansed my sin and made me whole.

So I will tell of Your great love
Until I reach Your home above.

IN OBEDIENCE TO YOU, LORD

In obedience to you, Lord,
I'll follow where you guide.
I'll have no fears, no doubts or cares
For you are by my side.

In obedience to you, Lord,
I'll love my fellow man
And tell at every moment
God's great salvation plan.

In obedience to you, Lord,
I'll remember that you said -
All those who don't call on your name
Remain forever dead.

In obedience to you, Lord,
I'll show the lost their need.
I know without you in my life,
I just could not succeed.

In obedience to you, Lord,
I'll walk your narrow path
And never turn aside, Lord,
Until my time on earth is past.

I know that in my own strength, Lord,
There's nothing I can do
Unless I live my life your way,
In obedience to you.

I SAW THE HOLY CITY

"I saw the Holy City, the new Jerusalem, coming down
out of heaven from God, prepared as a bride beautifully
dressed for her husband. And I heard a loud voice
from the throne saying, "Now the dwelling of God
is with men, and he will live with them. They will be
his people, and God himself will be with them and
be their God. He will wipe every tear from their eyes.
There will be no more death or mourning or crying or
pain, for the old order of things has passed away."

Revelation 21: 2-4 NIV

I looked towards the clouds and saw
The Holy City descend.
It was the new Jerusalem;
God's kingdom without end.
The Holy City was as a bride
Arrayed for her husband dear.
Then from the throne I heard a voice
And it echoed loud and clear.
It said that God now dwelled with men,
And among them He would live.
That they would be His people
And His protection He would give.
There will not be a tear to wipe,
For He's wiped them all away.
There'll be no death or mourning,
No crying or no pain.
For the old order has passed away;
It will be seen no more.
And God to all His people
Will His grace and love outpour.
The saints will watch from heaven's door
As all these things take place,
Secure in their salvation true
All thanks to God's great grace.

IT MAKES SENSE

Almighty God and gracious King
My praise will rise to thee.
When I but look around me here,
Your creation's all I see.

I see the flowers in bright array
And the majestic mountains rise.
I see the birds and creatures wild.
I see the clear blue skies.
I see the wonder of life begin,
And your power in a stormy night.
I see the waves come crashing in
With power and with might.

I hear the song of the birds that fly
As they chirp their song of praise.
I hear the thunder in the night,
And laughter through the days.
I hear the wonder in a child's voice
When he finds a treasure rare.
I hear the tears of a broken soul
When it thinks there's none who care.

I feel the grass beneath my feet,
And the sand on a sheltered place.
I feel the cold of a winter's day
And the sun warm on my face.
I feel the hurt of a friend betrayed,
And the love of friends so dear.
I feel the faithfulness of you
As you walk beside me here.

Almighty God and gracious King,
I don't know how it can be -
How a fool can say "There is no God!"
When your creation's here to see.

I WANT TO BE JUST LIKE MY FATHER

I want to be just like my father,
To carry His name with great pride.
I want that the world sees Him in me
As in His great love I abide.

I want to be just like my father,
He's the model I want to portray.
His characteristics I cherish
I'll emulate throughout each day.

I want to be just like my father,
To care for the helpless and lost,
To do what is right and what's noble
Without ever counting the cost.

I want to be just like my father,
To forgive when I've been betrayed,
To not seek revenge when one hurts me.
He taught me that's the right way.

I want to be just like my father,
My father in heaven above,
To show and tell all of his goodness,
To tell the whole world of His love.

To tell of His grace and His mercy
Bestowed on all repentant hearts,
And the quiet assurance of heaven,
And the peace and the joy He imparts.

I WILL NOT BOAST

"But, "Let him who boasts boast in the Lord." For
it is not the one who commends himself who is
approved, but the one whom the Lord commends."

2 Corinthians 10:17-18 NIV

I will not boast in what I've done,
But what God's done through me.
My life's renewed and so I tell
His love to all I see.

I will not boast in who I am.
For without him, I am done.
I did not do it by myself
It was Jesus – God's own son.

I will not boast in what I own
For possessions can't define
The riches he has blessed me with,
All his grace and love divine.

I will not boast of all my plans
For none of mine compare
To the master plan God has for me
As he holds me in his care.

I will not boast and seek applause
From man here on this earth.
Instead, I'll wait to hear God say,
"Your place in heaven's reserved."

JESUS IS

Jesus is my Comforter;
I rest within His care.
There is no woe or circumstance
With Him I cannot share.
Jesus is my faithful Rock;
His faithfulness is true.
He is my strong and mighty tower
That I can run into.
Jesus is my Savior King;
He rescued my dark soul.
He washed me in His crimson blood
And made my spirit whole.
Jesus is my all in all;
On Him I can depend.
Of His great love and mercy,
I will never see an end.
Jesus is my Counsellor,
My Redeemer and my Lord.
I know that He'll do best for me
As I daily mind His word.
But best of all, I revel in
His love that never ends.
I love Him for just who He is-
My Savior, Lord and Friend.

JUDGE AND KING

"For the LORD is our judge, the LORD is our lawgiver,
the LORD is our king; it is he who will save us."

For the LORD is our judge, and He's given commands.
His decree is the rock upon which we must stand.
We must walk straight ahead, not to left or to right
To ensure that we'll see Jesus' glorious might.
He said if we follow His decrees and His way
Then in glory we'll stand and be able to say,
"My LORD is the one way; from this thought I won't budge.
He has given commands, for the LORD is our judge."

For the LORD is our king; it is He who will save
Our souls from damnation, and our souls from the grave.
No power here in this world, no man, king or throne
Can make us deny that the LORD is our own.
For He loved us so much that He went to the tree
And shed His dear blood there on dark Calvary.
In glory, we'll see Him; loud praises we'll sing.
And say, with rejoicing, "The LORD is our king."

LESSONS TO LEARN

These words are what the Lord says,
He who my soul redeemed,
"I am the LORD, your God and King.
My lessons you must heed.
I will teach you all my precepts;
Your best is my concern.
I'll direct you in the way to go.
My teachings you must learn.
My lessons may not always give pleasure;
Some may give pain,
But when the pruning is complete,
The flower blooms again.
The flower grows much better
When all the pruning's done.
It's greater gain was at the cost
Of what the gardener's done."
I, too, just like the flower,
Want to be better still.
I need obey and rest within
The Father's holy will.
I need to know that all the way
My LORD Redeemer shows
Will bring about my greater good.
This thought I truly know.
For God has said He will direct
My path, throughout my days,
And I will have assurance
Of the truth in what He says.

LET US FIX OUR EYES ON JESUS

"Let us fix our eyes on Jesus, the author and perfecter of our faith, who for the joy set before him endured the cross, scorning its shame, and sat down at the right hand of the throne of God."

Hebrews 12:2 NIV

Let us fix our eyes on Jesus,
Author and perfecter of our faith.
Who for the joy set before him
Endured that crucifixion day.
His scorn was heaped upon its shame,
No import held by him
For he knew it as necessity
To save man from his sin.
He also knew the grave could not
Contain his awesome power
And that same power was well revealed
In that resurrection hour.
He now sits down at God's right hand
Enthroned for time above.
All praise is due him for his grace
And his sacrificial love.
So, let us fix our eyes on Jesus –
To him our worship give.
Because of his great act of love
Forever we will live.

LORD, HEAR MY CRY

*Jabez cried out to the God of Israel, "Oh, that you
would bless me and enlarge my territory! Let your
hand be with me, and keep me from harm so that I will
be free from pain." And God granted his request.*

1 Chronicles 4:10 NIV

Like Jabez, let my cry be heard
That you would bless me and your word
Would let my territory grow
And to all people wondrously show
How blessed is one who claims to be
Your own, and knows soul's liberty.
Keep me from harm so that no pain
Will stop my work or dare constrain
What you have told each one to do.
This, Lord, today I ask of you.
Like Jabez, may you grant my wish
To have your favor like a mist
Fall on me in a show of grace
Until I have run life's full race.
And when my life on earth is done,
And your planned course for me is run,
Then may I know communion sweet
As we will walk on golden streets.
And in that time, Lord, by and by
I'll thank you that you heard my cry.

LORD, LEAD ME IN TRIUMPH

Lord, lead me in triumph throughout every day.
And help me to stand firm on your narrow way.
When wicked men purpose to cause me to fall,
I'll remember you're close by and on your name call.

Lord, lead me in triumph secure in the thought
Because of Christ's shed blood, I am ransomed and bought.
There's no earthly treasure that means much to me
Compared to the great gift of my soul's liberty.

Lord, lead me in triumph, and help me to grow
More like you, Lord, daily. I want you to know
That you are the model on which I will base
My thoughts, words and deeds as I rest in your grace.

Lord, lead me in triumph; I'll not count the cost
Remembr'ing your torturous death on the cross.
No matter what trials and tests I go through,
Help me to keep focused on you, Lord, just you.

Lord, lead me in triumph and I'll follow along
And praise you forever in words and in song.
I'll proclaim to the nations your love and your grace
'Til my soul slips this earth and we meet face-to-face.

LOVE BECAUSE GOD LOVES US

"Dear friends, since God so loved us, we also ought to love one another. No one has ever seen God; but if we love one another, God lives in us and his love is made complete in us."

1 John 4:11-12 NIV

Since God so loved us from the start,
So we must love each other.
Each person that we meet each day
Is our sister or our brother.
And creed or colour can't dictate
The way we show our love.
Our greatest model is our Lord
Who came from up above
And took the sins of all mankind
Upon his lash-scarred back.
Without His willing sacrifice
We'd all know heaven's lack.
And though no one has seen God,
In believers He still lives.
His love is made complete in us
The more love that we give.

LOVE LETTERS

She opened up the dresser drawer
And pulled the package out.
A pack of letters, tied in red,
Of great value, there's no doubt.

She slowly loosed the ribbon
And took the letter off the top.
She read the words all written there.
Her tears just couldn't stop.

The words were written years before
And spoke of deep, abiding love
By the husband who had lost his life
His loyalty to prove.

He'd died to save his buddies;
He'd never had a second thought.
And so he yielded up his life
And his comrades' lives he'd bought.

Each time she read those letters,
She recalled the times they'd shared.
And now the words upon each page
Showed how deeply he had cared.

I also have love letters.
They too are tied with red-
The blood of Jesus Christ, my King,
As on the cross He bled.

The words are in the Bible,
And seen in every line
Are words of deep, abiding love
For He died to save mankind.

I too recall the times we shared
In joy, distress and grief.
And I cannot stop my own tears
For I can scarce believe

That the King of Glory came to earth,
A tiny baby boy,
Who died on Calvary once, for all,
To bring me peace and joy.

To give me life abundantly,
To stay right by my side
And as I read those words of love,
I pray I will abide

Within those loving arms of Christ
Who loosened all my fetters.
I've just to open the Bible up
And read my Lord's love letters.

MERE MORTALS CANNOT HARM ME

In God, whose word I praise— in God I trust and
am not afraid. What can mere mortals do to me?

Mere mortals cannot harm me
For I rest within God's care.
No matter where I go on earth,
My Savior God is there.
No earthly one possesses power
To snatch me from His hand;
My life is ruled by His great power
And all-sufficient plan.

Mere mortals cannot harm me
For in God alone I trust,
Not in the earthly things I know
That will decay and rust.
Not in a throne or kingdom,
Nor in scientific facts.
I trust in God alone because
I know His power will last.

Mere mortals cannot harm me
And won't cause my heart to fear
For this I know and won't forget –
My Savior's always near.
Time will not separate us
And no distance can distill
Our truly sweet communion
As I rest within His will.

Mere mortals cannot harm me
And can't fear around me raise;
It's God alone in whom I trust,
And whose word I ever praise.
For if my God be on my side,
With His great power and might
Why would I quake when mortal man
Can never win the fight?

MY HEART

My heart will sing a song of praise
And worship to its king will raise
For sins forgiven, sins atoned
For never walking all alone.

My heart that's cleansed from evil sin
Will have full joy well up within
And overflow so all I meet
Will know that God made life complete.

My heart that yielded to the cross
Was sentenced to eternity's loss,
But Christ, in love, took all my shame
And now eternity I can claim.

My heart that Satan made his own
Was cleansed, like snow, when love was shown
At Calvary's cross, when blood flowed free.
Christ hung and bled and died for me.

My heart will never understand
Why Jesus Christ, for sinful man,
Died on the cross God's will to do.
He died for me; He died for you.

My heart has finally found its worth,
And so for all my time on earth,
My heart will sing a song of praise
And worship to its king will raise.

MY SAVIOR! MY LORD! MY KING!

You sit at the Father's right hand
Having fulfilled God's salvation plan
To save the world's lost, fallen man
My Savior! My Lord! My King!

The glory of God, through you, shows
You have vanquished all of your foes.
Man your eternal power now knows.
My Savior! My Lord! My King!

Your word holds the power to sustain.
By your word was the world ordained.
You'll forever in majesty reign.
My Savior! My Lord! My King!

You're the One who defeated the grave
You suffered and died so you'd save
My repentant heart that I gave
To my Savior! My Lord! My King!

MY SIN WAS THERE AT CALVARY

My sin yelled loudly, "Crucify!
Give us the King of Jews."
My sin was pleased when Pilate said,
"I give him now to you."
My sin took scourge and struck your back
And yielded it with strength.
Your blood ran red and cruel stripes
Were shown on your back's length.
My sin took thorns and formed a crown,
And then mocked you as king.
Your blood ran down your holy face.
You did not do a thing!

My sin chopped down the cruel tree
And hewed the timbers rough.
My sin then formed them in a cross.
Yet, it was not enough.
My sin then placed your arms outstretched
And nailed them to the tree.
And then your feet were nailed as well.
You hung so willingly.
My sin heard the last breath you drew;
You whispered, "It is done!"
My sin took spear and pierced your side
To prove that you were gone.

My sin helped roll the stone in place;
It triumphed for the win.
No more would it hear that
It was conceived in Adam's sin.
But in that resurrection hour
When you rose up from the grave,
Despite what my sin did to you,
You knew it must be saved.
You'd done the Father's holy will,
By hanging on that cross,

So hearts that would repent of sin
Wouldn't suffer heaven's loss.

I should have hung there on that tree
Until I'd paid the price
Of all the debt my sins incurred,
And yet you sacrificed
Your own life for a sinner's debt.
You did not count the cost;
For without blood poured out for me,
My dark soul would be lost.
My sin, so grievous, mean and cruel
Was forgiven by your grace.
My heart, all new and freshly cleansed,
Could claim its royal place.

What love drove such a sacrifice
In a death so filled with pain?
What grace was there that was bestowed
To cleanse my heart again?
What mercy was displayed that day
As you hung on Calvary's tree?
Why was my sin so on your mind
That you gave your life for me?
How can I ever thank you, Lord,
For what you've given me:
A heart restored, a life renewed,
And my soul's liberty?

NO POWER ON EARTH

For I am convinced that neither death nor life, neither
angels nor demons, neither the present nor the future,
nor any powers, neither height nor depth, nor anything
else in all creation, will be able to separate us from
the love of God that is in Christ Jesus our Lord.

Romans 8:38-39 NIV

My heart is now convicted
That there's nothing on this earth
That will ever separate me
From the God who gives me worth.

No angel has the power,
No demon has the might
To ever separate me
For I rest within God's sight.

The present cannot do it;
The future time as well
Can't cleave the close communion
Since God saved my soul from hell.

No distance separates us;
No depths can ever cleave
For I know that Christ has saved me
And that He will never leave.

On this earth, there is not one thing
That can lure me from His hand
For God's love is all-sufficient.
This great truth I understand.

And I rest beside quiet waters
With the knowledge that's so great
That there's nothing in existence
That me, from God, can separate.

O LORD, MY GOD

O Lord, My God, I take refuge in you.
Save and deliver from all who persue.
Like a lioness, they will tear me to shreds
With no one around to save me from dread.

O Lord, My God, if there's guilt on my hands
If I've done any harm to a peace-seeking man,
If I have stolen, without cause, from my own foe,
Let them chase me and catch me and not let me go.

O Lord, My God, arise in your wrath
Directly please stand in my enemies' path
And let justice prevail in your power and might
So my enemies will be removed, like a blight.

O Lord, My God, let your people gather round
And guide them and lead them with principles sound.
You will rule over them from your vantage on high
And your people will know that your judgment is nigh.

O Lord, My God, with your righteousness true
Judge me and let me be reconciled to you.
O righteous God, who searches all hearts and minds
Destroy any wickedness that you can find.

O Lord, My God, make the righteous safe.
My shield, God Most High, deserves all my praise.
The righteous are saved from his wrath every day
If they will remain on the Lord's narrow way.

O Lord, My God, if you do not relent,
You'll sharpen your sword and your bow will be bent.
You'll prepare deadly weapons and arrows of flame.
And aim them at those who do not know your name.

O Lord, My God, if a man would give life
To evil and trouble, he'd suffer great strife!
If a man would dig holes and scoop the dirt out
He'd fall in it himself, of that there's no doubt.

O Lord, My God, the trouble he causes will fall
On his own head, there's no doubting at all.
The trouble he creates will recoil back on him
And you'll judge him because of his evil and sin.

O Lord, My God, I will always give praise
Because of your righteousness and your holy ways.
And anthems of praise will I send t'wards the sky
And will glorify always the Lord, God Most High.

PRAY FOR THE PRODIGAL

Pray for the prodigal
Who has wandered astray,
Who's been lured by the world
And its self-centred ways.

Pray for the prodigal
That the truth will be found
Of our Father in heaven
Whose great love abounds.

Pray for the prodigal
That the knowledge will come
Of the joyous reunion
That awaits him at home.

Pray for the prodigal
And don't stop your prayers
For God's timing is perfect.
Man's time can't compare.

Pray for the prodigal,
When he finally decides
That the way of the world
Cannot satisfy.

Pray for the prodigal
As he yields up his heart
And a new life in Christ
From that moment will start.

PREPOSITIONS OF POWER

Through Him, I have salvation-
The free gift of His grace.
The hour I gave my heart to Him
Ensured eternal place.
His blood on Calvary's cruel cross
And His resurrection hour
Ensures I have availed to me
His righteousness and power.

In Him I've quiet assurance
Where I'll spend eternity.
I know a mansion, robe and crown
Have been prepared for me.
I know that I will spend that time
In praise with saints before,
And once I reach His holy side,
I'll stay forevermore.

With Him, I have no need to fear
For what can mere man do?
I know I've access to His power,
His grace and mercy, too.
I rest within His loving care
Within His holy hand.
I rejoice in the peace I know
That believers understand.

For Him, I'll live my life on earth;
I'll walk His narrow way.
I'll show His love to those I meet
On life's path every day.
I'll tell them of God's love so deep
That man can't understand.
I'll forgive hurts and show them grace
For that's God's way and plan.

These prepositional words are full
Of love and power and hope.
Throughout my daily walk of life
They help me, each day, cope
With all the situations
In each minute of each hour,
For each one has a meaning
And is full of God's own power.

QUESTIONS AT THE PEARLY GATES

The man walked up to the pearly gates
And said, "Please let me in."
The Lord said, "First, please answer this
Before you go within.
Did you use the goods I had bestowed,
When orphans and widows called?
Did you feed the cold and hungry?
Did you think of them at all?
Did the poor come to your mind, Sir?
Did you give them clothes and shoes?
I'll let you enter, just respond.
On earth, what did you do?"
The man could only hang his head.
He knew what he had done.
He had no words to justify
His actions to God's Son.
He'd sat before a table full
Of all that man could need,
And never thought of all the poor
And how many he could feed.
He'd worn the finest clothes and shoes;
Of money. he'd no lack.
He'd never once considered those
Who wore tatters on their backs.
What could he say to God's own Son?
He could not form a thought.
He now would know the consequence
Of what his selfish life had bought.
His punishment would be the flames
In hell that can't be quenched,
And no communion with God's Son
'Til eternity comes to end.

61

REWARD FROM GOD

"So do not throw away your confidence; it will be richly rewarded. You need to persevere so that when you have done the will of God, you will receive what he has promised."

Hebrews 10:35-36 NIV

Confidence shouldn't be thrown away,
The confidence you have in the Lord,
For if you move on and persevere
You will receive a great reward.

When you have done the will of God
With striving and with love,
You will receive the promises
From your Father up above.

The owner of a thousand cattle
Upon a thousand hills
Will always keep you in His care
And His promises fulfill.

So great are His resources!
His grace and mercy, too!
No one could ever outgive God
When he bestows rewards on you.

SATAN, I'M YOUR SLAVE NO MORE

Satan, I'm your slave no more;
My soul has been set free.
The precious blood of Christ, my King,
Ran down from Calvary's tree.

Satan, I'm your slave no more;
I live without despair.
My Lord has given me new life
And I rest within His care.

Satan, I'm your slave no more;
My heart is full of love
Bestowed on me, with mercy too,
By my Savior up above.

Satan, I'm your slave no more;
Christ's blood has made me whole.
No longer will I see a time
When you control my soul.

Satan, I'm your slave no more;
Your end has been ordained.
Christ is the victor over you,
And I win in Jesus' name.

Satan, I'm your slave no more;
Don't bother coming around.
My life for all eternity
Is in my Savior found.

SERVICE AND SUFFERING

Now I rejoice in what was suffered for you, and I fill
up in my flesh what is still lacking in regard to Christ's
afflictions, for the sake of his body, which is the church.

Colossians 1:24 NIV

Lord, count me worthy to share in your pain
Secure in the knowledge that you rose again.
I'll be your eyes to discover the need.
I'll be your arms and I'll be your feet.

I'll love your people as your Word tells me to
I'll try in each case to do just what you'd do.
To love without knowing I'll be loved in return,
To tell everybody of your lessons I've learned.

I'll tell them the story of my life renewed
When burdens were lifted and your love I knew.
I'll tell them that they too can have this great gift
If only they'll repent and in your true way live.

But if I am chosen to be rejected and spurned
When I tell of your goodness. Then this I have learned
That, secure in the knowledge of what I have gained,
I rejoice I was worthy to share in your pain.

STAND STRAIGHT IN THE FIGHT

Stand straight in the fight
For our God is beside you,
He'll never forsake you
For his promise is true.
When triumph is distant
And hope seems to be lost
Remember that Satan
Lost the war at the cross.

When doubts, fears and worries
Bring you to your knees
Remember that our God,
On high, all things sees
And protects all his children
With his mighty power.
He'll be right beside you
In your darkest hour.

So no matter what happens,
Let your heart be at peace
Remember your Father
And his love that won't cease.
So, run into the battle;
And stand straight in the fight
For your victory's determined
By the Lord's strength and might.

STEWARD OF THE TRUTH

My Father gave a gift to me
And said, "Child, guard this well.
Don't let the world take it away.
Please do just what I tell."

Throughout my days, I've held it dear
And held closely to my heart.
I've shared it with some other folks,
Its goodness to impart.

The gift He gave was His own word,
The Scriptures, words so true
Of God's plan for salvation
To rescue me and you.

I know I've been entrusted
To pass on these great words –
The act of sacrificial love
By Jesus Christ, the Lord.

And when I share those golden words
I'm filled with grateful praise,
That Jesus, my Redeemer,
Bestowed on me His grace.

And when I walk this earth no more,
And stand before God's son,
I hope I hear my Savior say,
"Well done, my child, well done."

SUFFERING FOR CHRIST

"For it has been granted to you on behalf of Christ not only to believe on him, but also to suffer for him,"

Philippians 1:29 NIV

On Christ's behalf, you're given
A great and glorious gift.
That you must not only believe,
But to suffer all for Him.
When Christ redeemed you, Brother,
At no time did He ever say
That your life would have no trials.
He just asks you to obey
And to trust that He can give you
The strength to carry on
Until your walk is over,
Until your time is done.
The suffering is offered,
But not without reward
For when you walk in heaven,
In communion with the Lord,
You'll know it all was worth it,
You'll know your prize is won
For your time will be eternal
With the Father and the Son.

SUSTAINED AND SECURE

Even to your old age and gray hairs I am he, I am he who will sustain you. I have made you and I will carry you; I will sustain you and I will rescue you."

Isaiah 46:4 NIV

Even when you are aged,
And gray hair covers your head,
I alone will sustain you.
By my hand, you will be led.
I formed you 'neath your mother's heart
Before your time on earth.
I knew you, loved you long before
Your mother gave you birth.
My grace sustained you all the days
Since you called on my name.
My love's been multiplied to you.
Your life's not been the same.
My grace was shown on Calvary's tree
When my Son died for you,
And each drop that he bled that day
Showed his great love, ever true.
My power is all sufficient;
You have access to it all
In day or night, the moment
That on my name you call.
There is no king or kingdom,
No principality,
Can ever pluck you from my hand,
If you abide in me.

THE BATTLE WITHIN

There is a battle raging;
The enemy's within.
The foe is my old nature
That wants to see me sin.
There are no guns or cannons;
No gunsmoke fills the air.
But deep within my soul of souls,
A battle's raging there.
The enemy's commander
Is leading the attack
And wants to see me falter
And stumble on life's track.
He watches when I waver
And hopes that I will fall,
But all his hopes are crumbled
When on Christ's name I call.
I know that when God's with me,
I cannot lose the fight
For with my Great Commander,
I've access to His might.
There is no king or kingdom,
And no army has the power
That I gained from my Savior
In His resurrection hour.
He saved me from damnation.
My soul now rests secure
And I will ever thank Him
For salvation that is sure.
I willingly surrendered
All that I was and hope to be
And gained the gifts, so freely given,
Of grace and liberty.
The enemy's been conquered,
But yet will try to take
My peace and joy forever
'Til he's cast in fiery lake.

He knows his time is counted,
For the victory has been won
But yet he seeks to claim all men
Until his time is done.
The battle rages day by day;
The foe will not concede.
I'll win the daily battle
If God's word is what I heed.
And as I become like Christ,
And rest within His will
I'll know, for sure, I'm doing right
When the battlefield is still.

THE CAPTIVE

The prison door was barred and locked,
And Satan held the key.
The prison was not brick and wood
But all that was in me.
Each block was built with deep despair,
And joined with fear and doubt.
The walls were high, and oh so strong.
I thought I'd not get out.
The outside world looked inside
And saw a picture fine,
But as I looked into the world
All misery was mine.
In deep despair, I shouted, "Lord,
I can't handle this alone.
Please help me break these prison walls
And lead me to my home."
I wondered if He'd see my tears,
Or hear my heartfelt plea.
And then He came and brought along
His glorious liberty.
My chains fell off, no captive I,
He'd done it for my sake.
The key was snatched from Satan's hands
And the walls began to shake.
And as the walls came tumbling down,
And I stepped beside my King,
My voice rang out with songs of praise;
I could do naught but sing.
"I thank you, Lord, for who you are
And what you've done for me.
Your power has broken Satan's hold,
And you've set this captive free."

THEY SAY; THEY SAW

They say that you were a teacher,
Or maybe a preacher of fame.
The blind gained sight and the lame walked -
By the people you were acclaimed.
They saw just your deeds and actions
With no thought of the power within.
The leprous bodies were cleansed, Lord,
Like you cleansed my own soul from sin.
They saw you on Calvary's cruel cross,
And saw as you gasped your last breath.
They saw as the soldier drew his sword
And pierced your dear side to prove death.
They say that you fainted on that cross;
You slept deep but you did not die.
They say that your loving disciples
Took your body and told all a lie.
They say there was no resurrection,
That you lived and died here on earth.
They dismiss the power you displayed, Lord,
As they dismiss your miraculous birth.
But there will come a time in the future,
With all others in one accord,
They will stand in judgment before you
And will proclaim you, dear Jesus, as Lord.
And it's then that they'll see their Creator
And they'll know what they knew not before.
That the one that they said had no power
Is the King who will reign evermore.
They will see that their fate's been determined
That the fiery hell flames await
And their choice while on earth had established
Their ignoble, unchangeable fate.

UNSURPASSED SACRIFICE

*"But he was pierced for our transgressions, he was
crushed for our iniquities; the punishment that
brought us peace was upon him, and by his wounds
we are healed. We all, like sheep, have gone astray,
each of us has turned to his own way; and the
LORD has laid on him the iniquity of us all."*

Isaiah 53:5-6 NIV

He was pierced for our transgressions.
He was crushed for all our sins.
The punishment that gave us peace
Was inflicted upon him.
By the wounds he suffered for us,
By those red stripes, we are healed.
And those red mankind-saving stripes
God's salvation plan revealed.
With our Adam-given nature
We, like sheep, have gone astray.
And each woman, man and even child
Has turned to his own way.
Upon his cross-bruised shoulders
Christ carried all our sins.
And God Jehovah mighty
Laid our iniquity on him.
I never could repay that debt;
He paid a debt he did not owe.
I'll never understand it
But this one thing I know.
With my last breath I'll thank him;
My praises will not end.
For what Christ did upon that cross,
I'll never comprehend.

WHAT CHRISTMAS REALLY MEANS

The world has all its symbols
Of what Christmas really means -
The Christmas gifts wrapped nicely
Beneath the Christmas tree,
The golden baubles on that tree
That gleam with sparkling light,
The hustle and the scurrying
To find the gift so right.
The singing of some carols
About a babe in manger bed,
Some angels, and some shepherds,
And magi the bright star led,
And the food upon a table
With family all around.
The world says that this is where
Their Christmas joy is found.

The symbols that I hold so dear
Are just the same as those,
But the significance I place on them
Is different, I suppose.
The meaning is not quite the same;
I see a different way.
The import of them more intense
Because of Christmas day.
I understand the meaning
O what happened that first morn
When Jesus Christ, our Savior,
Was in a stable born.
For nothing that the world owns
Can ever be so dear
As that first Christmas long ago;
It really has no peer.

The gift I think of Christmas Day
Was wrapped in swaddling clothes
And laid within a manger stall.
It was Jesus Christ God chose
To save mankind from all his sin.
Who knew within that babe
Dwelt mankind's true salvation?
He is the Truth, the Way.
There's other gifts I think of when
Each Christmas Day is hence -
The gifts of all the magi
Of gold, myrrh and frankincense.
Gifts they delivered to a king,
A prophet and a priest
To one who died and rose again,
Whose reign will never cease.

When I espy a Christmas tree,
With branches rich and green,
It brings to my mind, every time,
A totally different scene.
The tree I think of was not green,
No beauty was instlled.
It was the tree of Calvary
That topped Golgotha's hill.
It bore my Savior on its beams;
It bore His holy weight
So that my heart could be renewed
And cleansed from its sin state.
So when the world sees Christmas trees,
It cannot clearly know
That Christ would die upon a tree
God's precious love to show.

And all the baubles on the tree
That shine and gleam so bright
Could not compare to starry host
That appeared in the dark, dark night.
When shepherds heard a heavenly choir
That loudly did proclaim
The birth of Jesus, Christ and King,
When to our earth He came.
They told the shepherds of His birth,
In lowly manger laid,
That He had come to earth and that
Sin's penalty He'd pay.
So please remember what it means
As you those carols sing –
The stars and heavenly choir
And the birth of Christ, the King.

And when I think of family,
I thank God for those I love;
I know that each one is a gift
From my Father up above.
I know that I'm a child of God;
I know that He loves me
And no barter, trade or purchase
Can get you this family.
But you'll be welcomed joyfully
When on Christ's name you call
If you'll admit you're a sinner,
He'll be your all in all.
You'll have a brand new family
To love and be loved by
And be joined forever beyond death
When to heaven your soul will fly.

WHEN MARY LOOKED AT JESUS

When Mary looked at Jesus
In that far-off holy land
She knew her child had power and might
With angels at His command.

When Mary looked at Jesus
She knew He held the key
To all the world's mysteries
And all knowledge man would need.

When Mary looked at Jesus
In his manger bed, so still,
She saw the world's Redeemer
And all prophecy fulfilled.

When Mary looked at Jesus
She saw what man can't see
And knew that ancient prophecy
Said He'd die on Calvary's tree.

So she held Him close and loved Him
As she held Him on her knee,
And knew that she'd lose Him here on earth
But He would open eternity.

So now, dear friends, use Mary's eyes
To look at Christ, the Lord.
Who came to earth as a human babe
But is the true, dear son of God.

And His name is Emmanuel, God with us
Wonderful Counselor, and Prince of Peace,
Mighty God, Everlasting Father.
Whose love will never cease.

YOU GIVE ME MORE

You gave me my home
And the clothes on my back.
Of material things
I scarce know a lack.

And yet when I ponder
And total the score,
I can't help but notice
You give me much more.

You give me your love
I know never ends.
You give me the gift
Of my family and friends.

You give me uniqueness
From each one on earth.
And what's yet more special
You've given me worth.

A person of value
You knew ere my start.
You formed me and made me
'Neath my mother's heart.

So thanks, Lord, for giving,
Abundant and free,
The person I am now
And the person I'll be.

YOU SING A SONG, LORD

You sing a song of love, Lord.
I hear it in the rippling brook I pass by on my way.
I hear it in the birds I hear around me every day.
I hear it in the laughter of my children as they play.
I hear it in the silence as their heads on pillows lay.
I hear your song of love.

You sing a song of care, Lord.
I hear it in the spoken word when people state we're free.
I hear it in the voices of friends you've given me.
I hear it in the comfort words when trials of mine they see.
I hear it in the shouts of joy when life's good as can be.
I hear your song of care.

You sing a song of creation, Lord.
I hear it in the canopy of green in forest dark.
I hear it in the melody of robin, jay and lark.
I hear it in the friendly wind that roams through field and park.
I hear it in growl of cats, and canine's warning bark.
I hear your song of creation.

You sing a song of sacrifice, Lord.
I hear it in the Bible when on that cross you died.
I hear it in the words that say they pierced your holy side.
I hear it in the thorny crown upon your brow they plied.
I hear it in your mother's voice as at your feet she cried.
I hear your song of sacrifice.

So let me be aware, Lord, of the songs you sing to me,
And let me share their melodies with others that I see.
Allow me to be grateful, Lord, for all the songs you sing,
And help me, Lord, throughout my life until to heav'n I wing.

YOU THOUGHT OF ME

You hung and bled on Calvary
But even in your agony
Your thoughts were only fixed on me
And my dark soul's eternal need.

You could have called your angel band
To lift you down and help you stand.
I know I'll never understand
Why you died to redeem man.

You suffered such a cruel end;
Your grace to man you did extend.
Your love, I know, will have no end
And on this truth I can depend.

And when you took your final breath
They thought that you'd succumbed to death.
For three days in the tomb you'd rest
Then from the grave the victory wrest.

You rose in triumph that third day
To heaven's gate, you showed the way
For those who walk your narrow way.
And on you daily their minds stay.

I thank you, Lord, for saving me
And winning me the victory.
Now joy and peace is all I see
From your name's call to eternity.

YOU WILL FIND ME

You will find me in the snow-capped mounts
That reach toward the sky.
You will find me in the unique sound
Each bird makes as it flies.
You will find me in the flowery glade
Where flowers show their hue.
You will find me in the babbling brook;
It sings my praise to you.
You will find me in a friendly smile,
A friend's smile from the heart.
You will find me in a friend's embrace
As your world is torn apart.
You will find me in a newborn's cry
And the parents' pure delight.
You will find me in the moon and sun,
And the inky starry night.
You will find me if your heart repents
And in truthfulness you seek.
You will find that I am faithful
And I'll be all that you need.